4

Powerful Spiritual Phrases That Can Change The Quality of Your Life

orkos press

THIS BOOK BELONGS

To:

Name:________________________________

40 Powerful Spiritual Phrases

ISBN: 1-59232-588-2

Orkos Press
New York

PRINTED IN THE UNITED STATES OF AMERICA

40 powerful spiritual phrases that can change the quality of your life

By Norman Vincent Peale

Edited by C. S. Moore

Also by Dr. C. S. Moore

1. My Favorite Bible Quotes
2. Remember How Far You Have Come
3. Who Moved My Cake
4. Where Have All Our Men Gone
5. Warrior of Conscience

CONTENTS

24. Have good intentions
25. Be forgiving
26. God is always in you
27. Have no doubt
28. Pray for your enemies
29. Stay resolute
30. Keep body and soul in order
31. Be not discouraged
32. Energize your life
33. Surrender to the lord
34. God has plans for you
35. Bring your burden to him
36. Keep your eyes on the prize
37. Project positivity
38. Seek the lord
39. Do not hate
40. You are saved

Since happiness and effectiveness depend upon the kinds of thoughts we think, it is absolutely impossible to be happy if we think unhappiness-producing thoughts. One of the wisest men who ever lived was Marcus Aurelius, who said, "A man's life is what his thoughts make of it." If you put into your mind thoughts of fear, you will get thoughts of fear out of your mind. Fill your mind with resentment thoughts, and resentment attitudes will emerge. And in neither case, of course, can you find happiness-inducing thoughts. Whatever the condition of your mind, the Thought Conditioners I am going to suggest are so powerful that they will displace unhealthy thoughts. Indeed, displacement is the only way you can drive a thought from the mind. In my experience through many years in working with people, I have discovered that the most vital, creative and positive thoughts are those stated in the Bible. Its words are alive. The Bible itself states what its spiritual words will do. “If ye abide in Me and My words abide in you ye shall ask what ye will, and it shall be done unto you.” This means, simply, that if you fill your mind with spiritual words so that they sink from your conscious to your subconscious mind by a process of spiritual osmosis, you will so condition your personality with spiritual power and sensitivity that God's will can operate in you.

Every great value of this life, the ones that really matter, shall then be yours. The words of the Bible are powerful Thought Conditioners. They are capable of revolutionizing the entire personality. Over the years, I had noticed that certain passages from the Scriptures had a particularly potent effect on human beings. I began, therefore, to list the life-creating words from the Scriptures that had done me the most good. Many of these I had recommended to others. Some of them had been called to my attention by people in whom there had occurred the most astonishing demonstration of new life and joy. When I applied them to myself, I found they did indeed possess tremendous effectiveness. The process I have used both personally and in counseling, which has accomplished most impressive results, is simply that of committing these great passages to memory. One puts them in the mind as in a sort of spiritual medicine cabinet, each to be drawn out as needed for specific ills or maladies of the personality, or to meet life's situations as they develop. As suggested above, the method is also to conceive of these thoughts as having displacement value, crowding out injurious thought patterns. The best results are gained by utilizing spare minutes to say these Scripture passages, or Thought Conditioners, over and over. As you are riding on a bus or train, or washing the dishes, or waiting for an appointment, utilize fractional moments to dwell and meditate upon the meaning of these texts. As you do so, there will flash out from them new insights, new perceptions of truth. Gradually, by a deep therapy, they will drive into the mind until presently your life will become a living demonstration of God's power. The booklet contains 40 creative and vital passages. Why 40? Perhaps because in His own deepest spiritual experience, Jesus spent 40 days in the desert withstanding temptation. There is no magic to the number 40, but it so happened that when I finished my list it totaled 40. There are many more vital passages. In fact, you can read and re-read the Bible for a lifetime and never exhaust its wisdom. This is my 40, and when you complete these and feel that they are in your permanent possession, explore the Scriptures further and find the many others that will have the same health-giving effect in your life. Now, the method for using this booklet: 1. I suggest that you read it through quickly at one reading to get the over-all impact of 40 of the greatest gems of thought ever spoken. 2. Start at the beginning and memorize one verse a day. Meditate upon the brief message given with each. Then practice the simple techniques suggested. 3. It may be that one or two or more of these will have a particularly strong effect upon you. In that case, I suggest that you remove it from the book, put it in your pocket, under the glass of your desk, or on your dressing table so that you can see it every day and thus it can become your dominating thought. These are not arranged according to problems or categories. Neither are they selected on any basis of relative importance. I have listed them just as they have come out of my own mind, one after the other. Perhaps God sorted them for this particular purpose. I give them to you with the prayer that these brief spiritual Thought Conditioners may add to the happiness and usefulness of your life.

1.

The things, which are impossible with men are possible with God. —Luke 18:27

This text shows how to do an "impossible" thing. Size up your problem, pray about it, do all you can about it. If it seems impossible, don't give up, but affirm, "The things which are impossible with men are possible with God." Keep relaxed. Don't worry. Avoid getting panicky. Never think, "This can't be done." Declare, "It can be done, it is being done because God is doing it through me." Affirm that the process is in operation. The final outcome may not be entirely what you now desire. But, handled in this manner, the solution will be what God wants it to be.

2.

Peace I leave with you, My peace I give unto you: not as the world giveth unto you. Let not your heart be troubled, neither let it be afraid. —John 14:27

Without a deep inner state of quietness, one becomes prey to tension, worry, and ill health. A song, a sunset, moonlight, the sea washing on a sandy shore, these administer a healing balm. But they lack power to penetrate the inner recesses of the soul. A profound depth therapy is required to attain healing quietness. An habitual repetition of this one text will, in time, permeate your personality with a complete sense of peace. When tense or restless, sit quietly and allow these words to pass unhindered through your thoughts. Conceive of them as spreading a healing balm throughout your mind.

3.

Renew a right spirit within me. —Psalm 51:10

Here is a fragment of a verse, which will bring you friends, health, happiness, and success. It can improve your disposition. The word disposition refers to the manner in which you are disposed to react to situations and people. If your automatic emotional reaction is irritable, crabby, selfish, haughty, it impairs or even destroys your relationships. The quality of your disposition depends upon your inner spirit. This thought conditioner, by the use of the word "renew," implies that when you were created, you had a good disposition. If you have allowed it to deteriorate, Almighty God, who created you, can recreate and renew in you the fine balance, the controlled spirit. He can restore that vital factor in a good disposition, inner quiet control. Let no day pass after today that you do not say many times, "Renew a right spirit within me."

4.

Come unto Me, all ye that labor and are heavy laden, and I will give you rest. —Matthew 11:28

Perhaps the strain and burden of life have made you tired. If so, maybe you are carrying life too heavily. Primarily, we do not get tired in our muscles but in our minds. We develop that "I'm swamped" feeling. Allow this text to dissolve in your thoughts as a kind of spiritual lozenge. As you turn to Jesus in your thoughts, He will give you rest. And how does He do that? One way is by showing you how to work. “Learn of Me,” He says. In other words, work by My method. "My yoke is easy, and My burden is light” (Matthew 11:30). That is to say, easy does it. Don’t strain, don't tug, relax. Do one job at a time using the light touch, the easy stroke.

5.

What things so ever you desire, when you pray, believe that you receive them, and you shall have them.
—Mark 11:24

To pray successfully, you must employ affirmation and visualization. Form a picture in your mind, not of lack or denial or frustration or illness, but of prosperity, abundance, attainment, health. Always remember you will receive as a result of prayer exactly what you think, not what you say. If you pray for achievement but think defeat, your words are idle because your heart has already accepted defeat. Therefore, practice believing that even as you pray you are receiving God's boundless blessings, and they will come to you.

6.

Trust in the Lord with all thine heart; and lean not unto thine own understanding. —Proverbs 3:5

This text will help you avoid a nervous breakdown. It will stimulate your recovery if you have had one. A famous neurologist, a specialist in nervous breakdowns often “prescribes” this text for his patients. He writes the words on a card and instructs his patient to commit them to memory and repeat them until they are indelibly printed on the subconscious mind. The cause of much nervous trouble is frustration. And the antidote to frustration is a calm faith, not in your own cleverness, or in hard toil, but in God’s guidance. The cure of frustration is the belief that God will help you obtain your heart’s desire. Trust in God with all your heart, and you will be able to keep on working in health and happiness for long years to come.

7.

I am come that they might have life, and that they might have it more abundantly. —John 10:10

Many people are lacking in energy. Their vitality is low. They are filled with inner conflicts, which dissipate energy. They are dull and apathetic. What is the secret of energized life? Christ is the answer. It is said of Him, "In Him was life" (John 1:4). Fill your mind with Christ, fill your heart with Him, and inevitably energy, vitality, exuberance, delight, and eagerness will well up within you. Every day as you repeat this text make it read, "Christ has come that I (fill in your own name) might have life and might have it more abundantly."

8.

Confess your faults one to another, and pray one for another, that you may be healed. The effectual fervent prayer of a righteous man availeth much. — James 5:16

God does heal. He does it in two ways, through science and through faith. In healing, confession is important, for much illness results from buried resentments and guilt. Confession to a competent counselor releases these poisons, cleanses the mind and soul, thus stopping the passing on of diseased thoughts to the body. Effectual prayer, that is scientific prayer, is very powerful. The essence of the technique is confess your faults, pray with kindred spirits even if separated by distance, and enthusiastically (fervently) believe.

9.

If God be for us, who can be against us? —Romans 8:31

Imagine yourself as actually looking at all your difficulties like an army lined up against you. Then realize you have a backing that can overcome them all. As you face these enemies of yours— discouragement, frustration, disappointment, hostility, weakness—ask yourself, "What shall I say to these things?" And the answer is, "If God be for us, who can be against us?" Now, spend a minute realizing that God is for you and say this affirmation: "God is with me. God is for me. God is greater than all these things." Then visualize these enemies of your peace and happiness as retreating, giving way before God's power. Personalize the text by saying: "If God be for me, who can be against me?" The repetitive use of this text will give you an enormous sense of God's presence and a powerful feeling of victory.

10.

The kingdom of God is within you. —Luke 17:21

When you are filled with self-doubt, and in the grip of your inferiority complex, don't give up saying, "I can't do it, I haven't it in me." You do have a very big "it" within you. You have the Kingdom of God within you. God has placed in your personality all the ability you need. You have only to believe in yourself, and strength within you will be released. In saying the text, try it this way, "God's abundance, peace, and power are within me. I lack for nothing."

11.

For God hath not given us the spirit of fear; but of power, and of love, and of a sound mind. —II Timothy 1: 7

Your fears can be healed by this text. It tells us, first, that fear is overcome by power. What power? There is only one force more powerful than fear, and that is faith. When fear comes to your mind, counter it with an affirmation of faith Second, love overcomes fear. By love is meant trust, confidence, complete dependence upon God. Practice this attitude and fear will diminish. The third element is to attain a sound mind in which there are no complexes, quirks, and obsessions. Live with the thought of God, and you will develop a sound mind where no shadowy fear can lurk. Whenever you are afraid, verbalize against the thing that you fear, using the words of this text.

12.

Thou shalt guide me with Thy counsel, and afterward receive me to glory. —Psalm 73:24

Perhaps, today, you have a problem, which has baffled you. Try allowing this text to penetrate your mind until it becomes a dominating conception, and it will do some important things for you. It will make you understand that there is an answer to every problem, and that God is thinking along with you. It will bring to bear upon your problem that keen and sharp perception of wisdom called insight. If you put every problem in God's hands, ask Him to give you the right answer, believe that He is doing just that, and will take the guidance that comes, your decisions will turn out right.

13.

Wherefore take unto you the whole armor of God that ye may be able to withstand in the evil day, and having done all, to stand. —Ephesians 6:13

This is one of the greatest of all techniques of mental health. It teaches that when we have done all that we can do about a given matter, we are not to get worried or in a panic or be filled with anxiety, but take a calm philosophical attitude concerning it. When you have done all that you can do, don't try to do any more, just "stand." Relax, stop, be quiet, don't fuss about it; you have done everything possible; leave the results to God.

14.

God is our refuge and strength, a very present help in trouble. —Psalm 46:1

When trouble strikes, what you want is comfort and protection. You want strength to stand up to it and meet it. You can have both. This text contains the answer. Frequently remind yourself that God is with you that He will never fail you that you can count upon Him. Say these words, "God is with me, helping me." This will give you a sense of comfort. New hope will flood your mind. New ideas will come. A new sense of power will be felt. As a result, you will rise above your trouble. When a particular trouble arises, before you do anything else about it, sit down quietly, repeat this text a half dozen times, and put your full faith in it.

15.

He that handles a matter wisely shall find good: and who trust in the Lord, happy is he. —Proverbs 16:20

To live successfully, one must overcome blundering ineptness, the tendency to do and say the wrong thing. One must develop the deft and skillful touch that makes things turn out right. A thing does not go wrong because of some perverse fate. It is more than likely that you lack the right slant, the proper approach. If such is the case, what you need is wisdom. If you let today's text seep from your conscious to your subconscious mind, it will correct the error pattern within you and gradually endow you with wisdom.

16.

Incline your ear, and come unto Me: hear, and your soul shall live. —Isaiah 55:3

Most people live on the surface. They miss the most astonishing things. They see and yet they do not see. And the reason is they aren't really looking. The same is true about what they hear. They listen with the outer ear, only. For example, people go to church, and the Gospel never penetrates beyond the outer consciousness. That is because people do not listen with all their faculties. They do not lose themselves in it. But when one inclines his ear and hears, listening as though his life depended upon it, getting every word, letting it sink into his mind by a deep and powerful penetration, then the message falls like a healing potency upon him. Every spiritual disease germ is killed, and he lives with new health and strength.

17.

Now unto him that is able to do exceeding abundantly above all that we ask or think, according to the power that work in us. —Ephesians 3:20

Today, remind yourself that nothing is too good to be true. Your great hopes can be realized. Your most wonderful dreams can come true. All that you really need, you can have. An incredible goodness is operating in your behalf. If you are living a paltry life, resolve to stop it today. Expect great things to happen. Confidently receive God's abundant blessings. Do not think lack. Instead think prosperity, abundance, the best of everything. God wants to give to you, His child, every good thing. Don't hinder His generosity.

18.

Ask, and it shall be given you; seek, and you shall find; knock, and it shall be opened unto you. —Matthew 7:7

This is a very practical technique of prayer. It works amazingly. One reason we do not get answers to our prayers is that we ask, but do not really expect to receive. We are expert askers, but inexpert receivers. This spiritual formula tells us to ask and then immediately conceive of ourselves as receiving. For example, to be free from fear, ask the Lord to free you. Then believe that He has immediately done so. The minute you express your faith by sincerely asking Him for a blessing and believe your prayer is answered, your prayer is answered.

19.

I have learned, in whatsoever state I am, therewith to be content. —Philippians 4: 11

Your present situation may not be to your liking. Perhaps you are dissatisfied and discouraged. Put the matter in God's hands. If He wants you elsewhere, He will lead you there, providing you are amenable to His will. But perhaps He wants you where you are. In that case, He will help you to adjust to the situation. He will make you content, even grateful for present opportunities. Learn the great art of doing the best you can, with what you have, where you are. When you do this, you learn how to reach the better condition, or how to make your present situation a better one.

20.

My soul, wait thou only upon God; for my expectation is from Him. —Psalm 62:5

One of the most serious and powerful facts in human nature is that you are likely to get what you are basically expecting. Spend years developing the mental attitude of expecting that things are not going to turn out well, and you are likely to get that result. You create a mental condition slanted to an unhappy outcome. If, on the contrary, you develop and maintain a mental attitude of faith and expectancy—hoping, dreaming, believing, praying, working—you will create conditions in which every good thing can and will grow. Fill your mind with the positive power of spiritual expectancy, and God and His good will flow toward you.

21.

Be strong and of a good courage; be not afraid, neither be thou dismayed: for the Lord thy God is with thee wherever you go. —Joshua 1:9

Here is a mental stimulus of tremendous power, which, if received and retained in your consciousness, will give you courage to overcome every difficulty. Nothing can ever dismay you. You may question whether mere words can accomplish so great a result, but never minimize the creative force of an active idea. A mental concept has more voltage than electricity; civilizations are changed by ideas. Emerson said, "Beware of an idea whose time has come."

22.

Be ye transformed by the renewing of your mind.

—Romans 12:2

People often manufacture their own unhappiness by the negative manner in which they think about things. Work with your mind, exercise disciplinary control, and re-slant your thoughts for happier living. Drain the mind, by consciously conceiving of yourself as dropping out every destructive thought, every fear, every inferiority feeling. Picture your mind as completely empty. Then start filling it with thoughts of God, and of Christ, thoughts about every good and pleasant thing. Practice this new habit regularly twice every day, morning and evening, to counteract the older and negative habit of allowing unhappy things to occupy your mind. In due course, unhappy thoughts will not feel at home in your mind, and happy thoughts will transform you.

23.

But as many as received Him, to them gave He power.

—John 1:12

You can possess within yourself all the power you will ever need in life. The method for securing power is very simple and depends entirely upon you. This text gives the formula: It is to "receive" Christ. When this is sincerely done, you will in turn receive power. And how do you receive Him? Simply decide that you want Him, tell Him so and mean it. Then, starting today, begin to live on a basis you know He would approve. The essence of the formula is surrender to God's will and Christ's way. It is the acceptance of a new manner of thought and life. Continue to re-surrender yourself every day, and in proportion as you do so, you will feel spiritual power surging in.

24.

The thing, which I greatly feared is come upon me, and that which I was afraid of is come unto me. —Job 3:25

This thought conditioner states a very serious warning. If, over a long period of time, a person habitually fears something, there is a tendency for that fear to become a reality. For example, if you fear that you are going to fail, and you constantly entertain thoughts of failure, you will create a mental condition that is propitious to failure. Creative, positive, success factors are repelled by your mind because your mind is filled with defeat attitudes. On the contrary, if you hold the faith thought, the positive thought, you will create about yourself an atmosphere propitious to success, health and wellbeing.

25.

This one thing I do, forgetting those things, which are behind, and reaching forth unto those things which are before, I press toward the mark for the prize of the high calling of God in Christ Jesus. —Philippians 3:13-14

Every person, if he is to have mental health and live successfully, must move away from past failures and mistakes and go forward without letting them be a weight upon him. The art of forgetting is absolutely necessary. Every night when you lie down to sleep, practice dropping the day into the past. It is over, finished. Look confidently to the future with God.

26.

In all these things we are more than conquerors through Him that loved us. For I am persuaded, that neither death, nor life, nor angels, nor principalities, nor powers, nor things present, nor things to come, Nor height, nor depth, nor any other creature, shall be able to separate us from the love of God, which is in Christ Jesus our Lord.

—Romans 8:37-39

These words mean that no matter what happens, nothing can separate you from God's love and protection. The secret is to build up in your mind, day by day, the knowledge and realization of God's presence and His love for you. Dwell on this mentally until it becomes an unshakeable fact.

27.

If any man thirst, let him come unto Me, and drink.

—John 7:37

Every now and then, deep unsatisfied longings well up within us. We may seem to have everything the heart can desire and ought to be perfectly satisfied. But still these vague dissatisfactions alloy our happiness. When you notice such feelings, try saying this verse a few times. As you do so, try to imagine how Jesus looked when He said these words: the kindness, the understanding, the peace on His face. Try picturing yourself as receiving from Him a drink of cold water— symbolic of the water of life that completely satisfies thirst so that one never thirsts again. Affirm that you receive from Him the ultimate in soul satisfaction. A deep inner peace will gradually grow upon you.

28.

Love your enemies, bless them that curse you, do good to them that hate you, and pray for them which despitefully use you, and persecute you. — Matthew 5:44

Make a list of all the people who have hurt and mistreated you or whom you do not like. Then pray for each by name and sincerely practice forgiving each one. Ask the Lord to bless them. Tell the Lord that you want to mean this. Repel the thought that after all you are "justified" in your resentment. Then speak kindly about these persons to others. Go out of your way to help them. This will, in time, break down many barriers, but even if it shouldn't, the effect upon you will be amazing. It will clear the channel through which spiritual power flows into you.

29.

I can do all things through Christ, which strengthens me.

—Philippians 4:13

This is an antidote for every defeat feeling. If you feel downed by situations, and the going is hard, this statement will remind you that you do not need to depend upon your own strength entirely, but that Christ is with you and is now giving you all the help you need. Teach yourself to believe that through Christ's help you can do all things. As you continue this affirmation, you will actually experience Christ's help. You will find yourself meeting problems with new mental force. You will carry heavy burdens with ease. Your new "lifting" power will amaze you.

30.

In Him we live, and move, and have our being.

—Acts 17:28

This text is a formula for maintaining physical, mental, and spiritual energy. The tension and pressure of modern living draws wearily upon our energies. But here we have a renewal method. The text reminds us that God created us and that He can constantly and automatically re-create us. The secret is to maintain contact with God. This channels vitality and energy and constant replenishment into our being. Every day, preferably about mid-afternoon when an energy lag usually comes, try repeating this text while visualizing yourself as "plugged" into the spiritual line. Affirm that God's recreative energy is restoring strength and power to every part of your body, your mind, and your soul.

31.

If any man be in Christ, he is a new creature: old things are passed away; behold all things are become new.
—II Corinthians 5:17

Never be discouraged about yourself. You may have tried all your life long to rid yourself of your weaknesses, your obsessions, jealousies, sins, inferiorities, without success. Your failure is probably that you have been trying to make yourself over. That is a long, tedious, and essentially impossible project. But it can be done in no time at all by Christ. All you need do is to say to Him simply, "Lord, I do not want to be this way anymore," and mean it. He will do for you what you cannot do for yourself—effect a lasting change in you. Ask Him to change you.

32.

Whosoever shall say unto this mountain, be thou removed, and be thou cast into the sea; and shall not doubt in his heart, but shall believe that those things which he saith shall come to pass; he shall have whatsoever he saith.

—Mark 11:23

Almost alone this passage can revolutionize your life and change defeat into victory. What does it tell you? That your "mountain," that great rock—like obstruction, that tremendous barrier, can be broken down and ousted from your life. You must not doubt "in your heart." Allow no negative thoughts to exist in your subconscious mind. Pray that your mountainous difficulty shall be removed and, as you pray, believe that it is being done then and now. Don't have the hazy idea that "this mountain" may be removed sometime in the future, but believe that God is removing it for you now.

33.

They that wait upon the Lord shall renew their strength; they shall mount up with wings as eagles; they shall run, and not be weary; and they shall walk and not faint.

—Isaiah 40:31

This beautiful sentence describes the greatest experience that can ever happen to you. It is called spiritual experience. You get it by completely surrendering yourself to God, and experiencing His presence. Then the heavy weights of your life drop away, and you are lifted to eagle-like levels of freedom and power. But no one can permanently live in such exalted emotional heights. Nevertheless, the power stays with you so that you can move through life with a speed and strength you never had before; you can "run and not be weary." Then even when you get up against day-by-day situations that used to be difficult and monotonous, this power is so great that it keeps you going without depletion of strength. Spiritual experience begins by lifting you to new high levels, after which it helps you to keep going with continuous power.

34.

Eye hath not seen, nor ear heard, neither have entered into the heart of man, the things which God hath prepared for them that love Him. —I Corinthians 2:9

Possibly life has become difficult—even dismal. You may not be getting zest or thrill out of living. The text for today will restore the old delight in life. It tells you that you have never seen, nor heard, nor even imagined all the marvelous, amazingly fascinating things that God will do for those who love Him, trust Him, and put His principles into practice. As you surrender your life to God, every experience of living will grow increasingly more wonderful.

35.

Cast thy burden upon the Lord, and He shall sustain thee: He shall never suffer the righteous to be moved.

—Psalm 55:22

A human mind can stand only so much weight. One mental burden piled upon another, unless relief is obtained, will in due course reach your breaking point and cause serious difficulty. Fortunately, you do not need to carry your burdens without assistance. God will help you carry them. But how is this done? It is accomplished in the mind. Practice thinking that God is actually with you. Tell Him about your burdens, and believe that He relieves and assists you. Form a picture of yourself as shifting your burdens to Him. He is willing to assume them and is perfectly able to do so. But, and this is most important, don't half give them. And don't take them back. Let God handle them. Leave them with Him.

36.

Thou wilt keep him in perfect peace, whose mind is stayed on Thee. —Isaiah 26:3

If your mind is filled with defeat thoughts, fear thoughts, resentment thoughts, you are bound to be in a state of mental unrest, even turmoil, and of course there can be no inner peace. This passage advises you to practice thinking about God, to keep your mind "stayed" or fixed, not upon your troubles but upon God. Keep your mind on God for as many minutes during the day as possible. This may be difficult at first for you are unused to spiritual concentration. Practice will make it easier.

37.

This is the refreshing. —Isaiah 28:12

These few words remind us of a spring of cool water because of their renewing quality. The frequent use of today's text has an invigorating effect. Sometimes, after a busy day or even in the midst of exacting activities, stop and say these words over to yourself and note how they dissipate weariness and refresh the body, mind, and spirit. The best method for using these words is to say them slowly, emphasizing their soft quiet melody. At the same time conceive of peace, rest, and renewal as coming to you.

38.

I sought the Lord, and He heard me, and delivered me from all my fears. —Psalm 34:4

A cure for fear that will absolutely work is to get close to God in your thoughts. He is the only certain unchanging factor in the world. He will never let you down nor forget you. If plagued by fear, do what this text says: "Seek the Lord." That may be done by spending 15 minutes every day just thinking about God. You can split this up into five minute periods, but never let a day pass without spending 15 minutes thinking about God. Each day, make the following statement, "I surrender myself and all my problems, my loved ones, my future into the hands of God, and I trust Him." Three times every day, thank God for all His goodness. Soon your life will be filled with God, and emptied of apprehensions.

39.

When ye stand praying, forgive, if ye have aught against any. —Mark 11:25

If you are not getting answers to your prayers, check yourself very thoroughly and honestly as to whether you have resentments in your mind. Spiritual power cannot pass through a personality where resentment exists. Hate is a non-conductor of spiritual energy. I suggest that every time you pray, you add this phrase, "Lord, take from my thought all ill will, grudges, hates, jealousies." Then practice casting these things from your thoughts.

40.

They shall hunger no more, neither thirst anymore; neither shall the sunlight on them, nor any heat. For the lamb which is in the midst of the throne shall feed them, and shall lead them unto living fountains of waters: and God shall wipe away all tears from their eyes.
—Revelation 7:16-17

This is one of the most comforting passages in all literature. It teaches that our loved ones are in a place of peace and beauty. They are under the watchful care of God and regularly experience His tenderness. The deep hunger and thirst of their souls has been satisfied. God, like a loving mother, puts His protection over them and with a kindly hand wipes away every tear from their eyes. This He has done for your dear ones who have crossed over to the other side. If you learn to love this passage and meditate upon it, He will wipe away every tear from your eyes, also.

Printed in Great Britain
by Amazon

33738108R00030